TEC

Count On It!
Four

¡Cuenta con ello!
Cuatro

Dana Meachen Rau

 Marshall Cavendish
Benchmark
New York

Four sides.

❖

Cuatro lados.

3

Four rings.

❖

Cuatro anillos.

Four legs.

—❖—

Cuatro patas.

Four wings.

—◆—

Cuatro alas.

Four frogs.

———❖———

Cuatro ranas.

Four bases.

❖

Cuatro bases.

13

Four buttons.

———❖———

Cuatro botones.

Four faces.

❖

Cuatro caras.

Four!

¡Cuatro!

19

Words We Know
Palabras conocidas

bases
bases

buttons
botones

faces
caras

frogs
ranas

legs
patas

rings
anillos

sides
lados

wings
alas

21

Index

Page numbers in **boldface** are illustrations.

Índice

Las páginas indicadas con números en **negrita** tienen ilustraciones.

About the Author

Dana Meachen Rau is the author of many other titles in the Bookworms series, as well as other nonfiction and early reader books. She lives in Burlington, Connecticut, with her husband and two children.

Datos biográficos de la autora

Dana Meachen Rau es la autora de muchos libros de la serie Bookworms y de otros libros de no ficción y de lectura inicial. Vive en Burlington, Connecticut, con su esposo y dos hijos.

With thanks to the Reading Consultants:

Nanci Vargus, Ed.D., is an Assistant Professor of Elementary Education at the University of Indianapolis.

Beth Walker Gambro is an Adjunct Professor at the University of St. Francis in Joliet, Illinois.

Agradecemos a las asesoras de lectura:

Nanci Vargus, Dra. en Ed. y profesora auxiliar de Educación Primaria en la Universidad de Indianápolis.

Beth Walker Gambro, profesora adjunta en la Universidad de St. Francis en Joliet, Illinois.

Marshall Cavendish Benchmark
99 White Plains Road
Tarrytown, New York 10591
www.marshallcavendish.us

Library of Congress Cataloging-in-Publication Data

Rau, Dana Meachen, 1971–
[Four. Spanish & English]
Four / by Dana meachen Rau = Cuatro / por Dana Meachen Rau.
p. cm. – (Bookworms. Count on it! = ¡Cuenta con ello!)
Includes index.
ISBN 978-0-7614-3476-4 (bilingual ed.) – ISBN 978-0-7614-3448-1 (Spanish ed.)
ISBN 978-0-7614-2969-2 (English ed.)
1. Four (The number)–Juvenile literature. 2. Number concept–Juvenile literature.
I. Title. II. Title: Cuatro.
QA141.3.R27618 2009
513.2'11–dc22
2008017236

Editor: Christina Gardeski
Publisher: Michelle Bisson
Designer: Virginia Pope
Art Director: Anahid Hamparian

Spanish Translation and Text Composition by Victory Productions, Inc.
www.victoryprd.com

Photo Research by Anne Burns Images

The photographs in this book are used with permission and through the courtesy of:
Corbis: pp. 1, 17, 20BL Tracy Kahn; pp. 3, 21BL Patricia McDonough/zefa; pp. 9, 21BR Robert Spoenlein/zefa; pp. 13, 20TL David Bergman. Jupiter Images: pp. 5, 21TR Jeffrey Allen Cable; pp. 15, 20TR Lilly Dong. SuperStock: pp. 7, 19, 21TL age fotostock; pp. 11, 20BR Mauritius.

Printed in Malaysia
1 3 5 6 4 2